W9-CCX-261

EDGE BOOKS

THE WORLD'S TOP TENS

The World's

DEADLIEST DISEASES

by Tim O'Shei

Consultant:
Nancy E. Freitag, PhD
Associate Member
Seattle Biomedical Research Institute
Seattle, Washington

Capstone
press

Mankato, Minnesota

Edge Books are published by Capstone Press,
151 Good Counsel Drive, P.O. Box 669, Mankato, Minnesota, 56002.
www.capstonepress.com

Library of Congress Cataloging-in-Publication Data
O'Shei, Tim.
    The world's deadliest diseases / by Tim O'Shei.
    p. cm.—(Edge Books. The world's top tens)
    Summary: "Describes in a countdown format 10 of the world's deadliest diseases"—
Provided by publisher.
    Includes bibliographical references and index.
    ISBN-13: 978-0-7368-5452-8 (hardcover)
    ISBN-10: 0-7368-5452-5 (hardcover)
    1. Medicine—Juvenile literature. 2. Diseases—Juvenile literature. 3. Communicable
diseases—Juvenile literature. I. Title. II. Series.
R130.5.O77 2006
616—dc22
                              2005019422

Editorial Credits
Angie Kaelberer, editor; Kate Opseth, set designer; Jenny Bergstrom, book designer;
    Kelly Garvin, photo researcher; Scott Thoms, photo editor

Photo Credits
AP Photo/Kenneth Lambert, 6, 26 (upper left); Sayyid Azim, 14, 27 (upper left)
Corbis, 16, 27 (upper right); CDC/PHIL, 13, 26 (bottom right); Gideon
    Mendel/ActionAid, 20, 27 (middle right); Reuters, 7, 18, 27 (middle left);
    Roger Ressmeyer, 24, 27 (bottom right); Sygma/Robert Patrick, 4;
    William Whitehurst, cover
Getty Images Inc., 12; AFP, 22, 27 (bottom left); Getty Images News, 25;
    Time Life Pictures, 10, 26 (bottom left)
Photo Researchers, Inc./LADA, 29; Martin Dohrn, 21; Simon Fraser/Royal Victoria
    Infirmary, Newcastle/Science Photo Library, 8, 26 (upper right)
Visuals Unlimited/Dr. Richard Kessel & Dr. Gene Shih, 9

TABLE OF

CONTENTS

DEADLY DISEASES

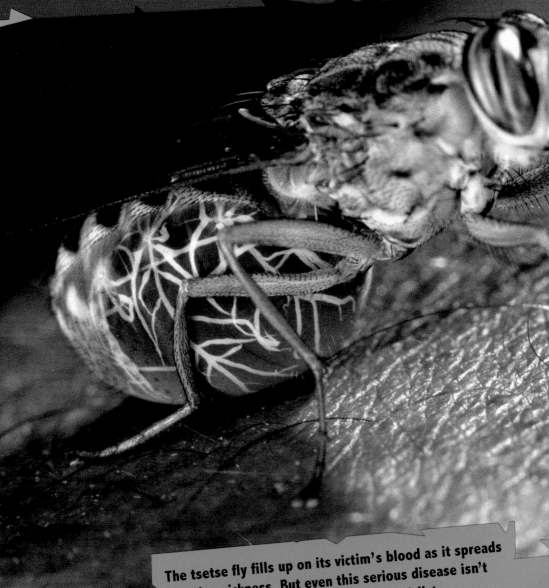

The tsetse fly fills up on its victim's blood as it spreads sleeping sickness. But even this serious disease isn't bad enough to earn a spot on our top 10 list.

Lots of things in the world are scary. Huge, hairy spiders. Sharks with rows of sharp, jagged teeth. Enormous grizzly bears. They're all enough to make the bravest person turn and run.

But what about the scary things you can't see? Germs float through the air and enter our lungs and blood. Tiny parasites feast on our skin. They cause diseases that make people very, very sick.

On the following pages, you'll read about the deadliest diseases on the planet. Many of them are rare. Most of them strike people in poor countries, where doctors and medicine are in short supply. But some of the diseases may be hiding in your backyard.

If you know about these germs, you'll be better prepared. So read on and learn. Some nasty germs are lurking out there!

10

ANTHRAX

Before 2001, anthrax was mainly a disease of farm animals. But that changed when an unknown person used anthrax as a weapon.

In late 2001 and early 2002, someone mailed envelopes filled with white powder. This powder contained anthrax spores.

People get anthrax in one of three ways. Touching the spores causes a small blister on the skin. With treatment, nearly all people who get anthrax this way survive. People who swallow the spores get bloody diarrhea and run a high fever. People who breathe the spores cough and have chest pain. About half of victims who swallow or breathe anthrax die.

4TH GRADE
GREENDALE SCHOOL
FRANKLIN PARK NJ 08852

SENATOR DASCHLE
509 HART SENATE OFFICE
BUILDING
WASHINGTON D.C. 2051

20510/4103

Many of the letters containing anthrax were sent to politicians. They were disguised as letters from kids.

VACCINE:	Being tested on U.S. soldiers
HOW IT SPREADS:	Touching, swallowing, or breathing anthrax spores
TREATMENT:	Antibiotics
2001 ANTHRAX ATTACK:	Five people died; the attacks remain unsolved.

7

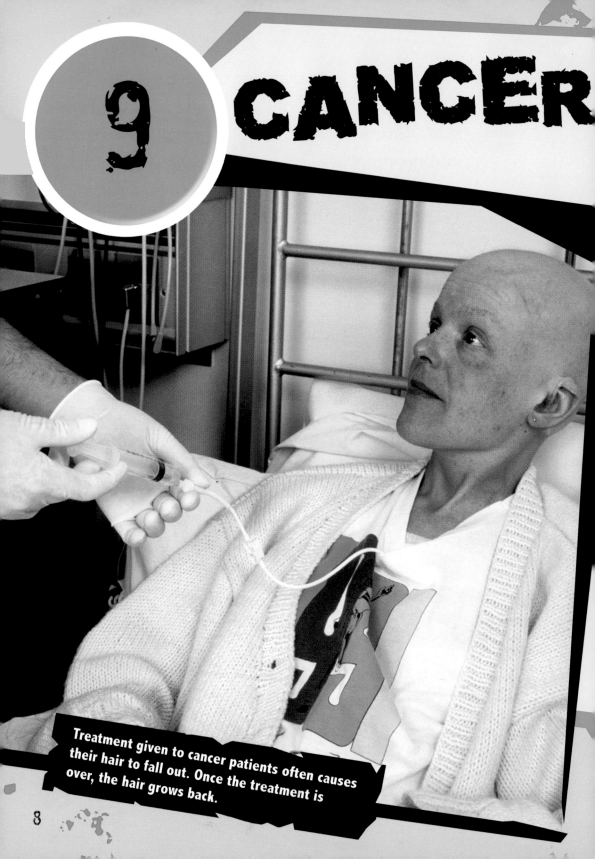

9 CANCER

Treatment given to cancer patients often causes their hair to fall out. Once the treatment is over, the hair grows back.

Cancer is one of the most well-known and common deadly diseases. Each day, it kills about 1,500 people in the United States alone.

Cancer is a disease of the cells. Cancer cells grow very fast. They destroy healthy cells.

Cancer is often first noticed as a tumor. This mass of cells bunches together to form a bumplike growth. Not all tumors are cancer. But anyone who thinks they may have a tumor should see a doctor. If doctors find cancer early, they can treat or remove the damaged cells and stop the disease from spreading.

Cancer cells divide and grow much more quickly than healthy cells do.

CAUSE: Damaged DNA in a cell

CAN IT SPREAD FROM PERSON TO PERSON? No

MOST COMMON: Lung cancer

MOST DEADLY: Lung cancer

TREATMENT: Surgery, medicine, or radiation

8

During the 1300s, plague victims were buried in mass graves called plague pits.

CARRIERS: Bubonic plague is spread by infected fleas; pneumonic plague is spread by people.

TREATMENT: Antibiotics

CASES TODAY: In the United States, 10 to 20 per year; 1,000 to 1,300 worldwide

MOST U.S. CASES: In the southwestern states, especially New Mexico and Arizona

PLAGUE

During the 1300s, plague was a terrible killer in Europe and Asia. Millions died. At least one-third of Europe's population was wiped out.

There are different kinds of plague. The type that swept across Europe is bubonic plague. It spread through the bite of infected fleas, which lived on rats. Europe's cities had huge rat populations during the 1300s.

The flea's bite contained bacteria that spread through the bloodstream, causing huge swellings in the neck, armpits, and groin. These swellings, which were as big as oranges, were called buboes. Sometimes the buboes burst, leaking blood and pus.

The victim's blood vessels also leaked, turning the skin dark. Because of this, people called bubonic plague the "Black Death." The buildup of bacteria in the bloodstream often killed the victim.

Today, plague is rare. Doctors treat it with antibiotics.

Painful pox cover a smallpox victim's skin.

SMALLPOX

At one time, smallpox was one of the world's most dreaded diseases. It killed millions of people throughout the world.

Smallpox started with a high fever and body aches. A few days later, small red spots filled the victim's mouth. Those spots spread to the face, arms, legs, and feet.

Next, those spots filled with fluid and grew into painful pox.

Three out of 10 victims died within two weeks. If the person survived, the pox became scabs and fell off about two weeks later. Survivors often had deep scars on their bodies. Some were left blind.

In 1967, a program began to vaccinate every person in the world against smallpox. By 1980, smallpox was considered wiped out.

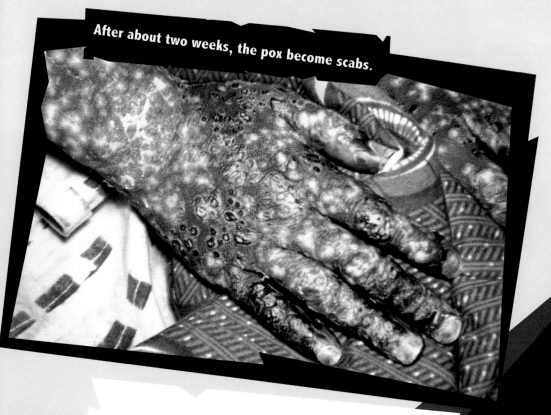

After about two weeks, the pox become scabs.

TREATMENT: None, but smallpox is prevented by a vaccine

SPREAD BY: Contact with an infected person

VACCINE: No longer routinely given, but governments keep a supply on hand in case of an outbreak

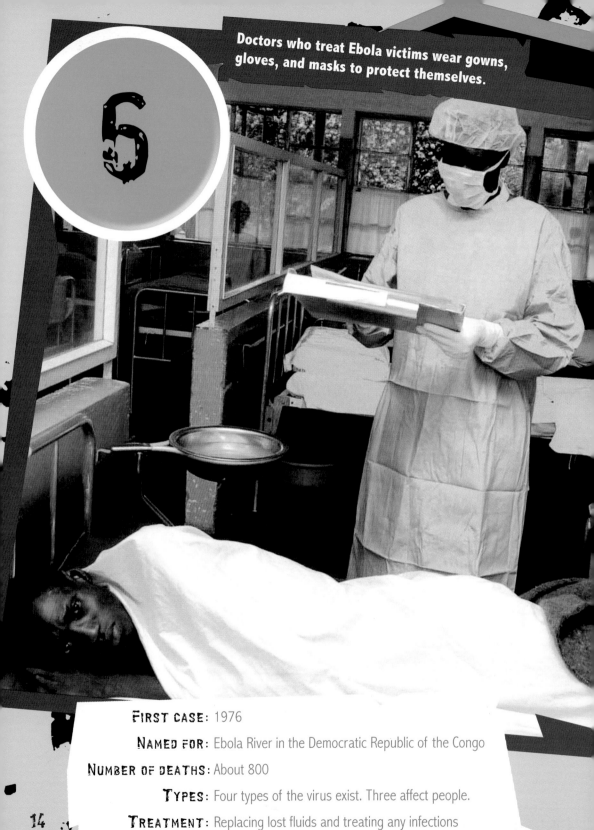

6

Doctors who treat Ebola victims wear gowns, gloves, and masks to protect themselves.

FIRST CASE: 1976

NAMED FOR: Ebola River in the Democratic Republic of the Congo

NUMBER OF DEATHS: About 800

TYPES: Four types of the virus exist. Three affect people.

TREATMENT: Replacing lost fluids and treating any infections

EBOLA

Ebola is one of the nastiest killers ever known. It causes its victims to bleed both inside and outside the body. The kidneys and liver bleed into the rest of the body. The person also bleeds through the mouth, nose, and eyes.

The blood of an Ebola victim is dangerous. It can spread the disease even after the person's death. Doctors and nurses who treat victims must wear masks and protective clothing.

Fortunately, the Ebola virus is not common. The disease mainly exists in jungle areas of Africa and is spread through animals.

In 1996, a group of people in Gabon, Africa, were hunting for food. They found a dead chimp and ate it. The chimp was infected with Ebola. Nineteen of the hunters got sick. So did 18 of their family members. More than half of the victims died.

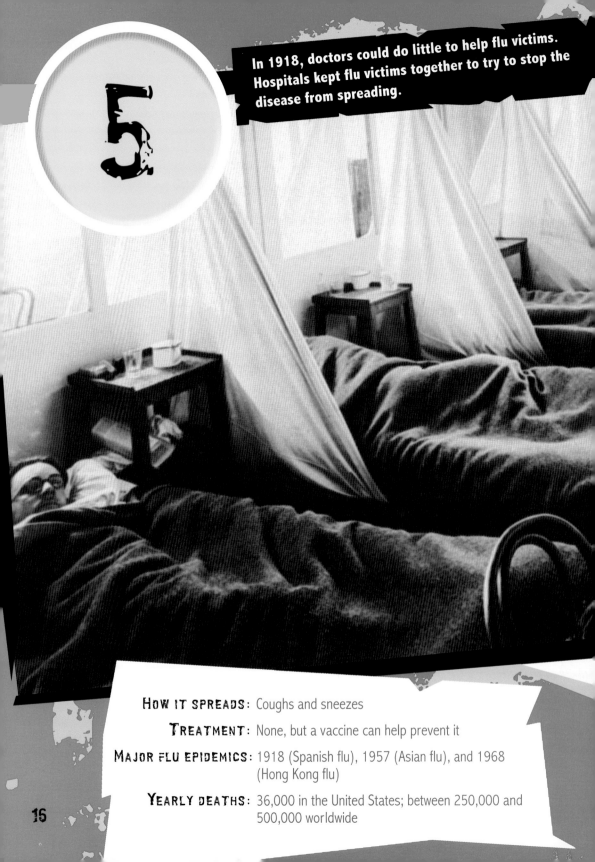

5

In 1918, doctors could do little to help flu victims. Hospitals kept flu victims together to try to stop the disease from spreading.

HOW IT SPREADS: Coughs and sneezes

TREATMENT: None, but a vaccine can help prevent it

MAJOR FLU EPIDEMICS: 1918 (Spanish flu), 1957 (Asian flu), and 1968 (Hong Kong flu)

YEARLY DEATHS: 36,000 in the United States; between 250,000 and 500,000 worldwide

INFLUENZA

Millions of people get the flu every year. It's so common that many people might not think it's a killer. But the flu can indeed be deadly. It is especially dangerous to people with asthma, diabetes, or heart problems.

The flu is a respiratory illness. It infects the nose, throat, and lungs. People with the flu have a hard time breathing. Their bodies ache. They may have a fever and feel very tired. A bad case of the flu can lead to pneumonia or dehydration. Many victims die when their lungs quickly fill with fluid, much like a person who drowns.

Each year, the flu kills about 36,000 people in the United States. That is more than the number of people who fit in most sports arenas. But past flu epidemics have been much worse. In 1918, the Spanish flu killed 675,000 Americans. At least 20 million people died worldwide that year.

Dirty drinking water can spread cholera.

CHOLERA

"**D**on't drink the water."
People who travel to South America,
Africa, and Asia often hear this advice.
Cholera is one of the main reasons.

In some countries, clean water isn't available. People use rivers or lakes as toilets. They also bathe in and drink from the same body of water. That dirty water is full of nasty germs. One of the nastiest causes cholera.

People with cholera lose body fluids through diarrhea and vomiting. These symptoms are treated by drinking a mixture of sugar water and salt water.

But treating cholera isn't always so simple. In rare cases, the symptoms are so severe that the person loses water too quickly. The victim goes into shock and dies within hours.

In countries where cholera is a threat, drinking bottled water is a must. So is cooking food completely. Your life depends on it.

HOW IT SPREADS: Food and water

OTHER CARRIERS: Cholera is sometimes found in shellfish, such as crab or shrimp.

TREATMENT: Replacing body fluids

CASES: Five or fewer cases in the United States each year

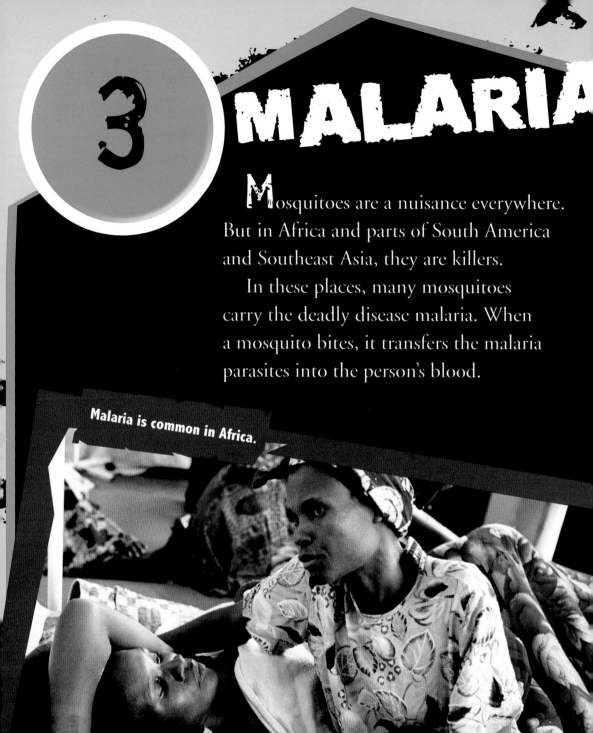

3 MALARIA

Mosquitoes are a nuisance everywhere. But in Africa and parts of South America and Southeast Asia, they are killers.

In these places, many mosquitoes carry the deadly disease malaria. When a mosquito bites, it transfers the malaria parasites into the person's blood.

Malaria is common in Africa.

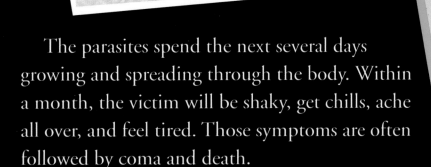

As it bites, the *Anopheles gambiae* mosquito injects the parasite causing malaria into the victim's skin.

The parasites spend the next several days growing and spreading through the body. Within a month, the victim will be shaky, get chills, ache all over, and feel tired. Those symptoms are often followed by coma and death.

Between 1 million and 2 million people die from malaria each year. Every 30 seconds in Africa, a child dies from malaria. Malaria can be treated when it is found early enough. But in poor countries where malaria is common, people can't afford the medicine.

CARRIER: The female *Anopheles gambiae* mosquito

CASES EACH YEAR: 1,300 in the United States; 500 million worldwide

DEATHS: Between 1 million and 2 million each year

U.S. NUMBERS: Almost all U.S. malaria victims get the disease while traveling overseas.

TREATMENT: Quinine and other medicines

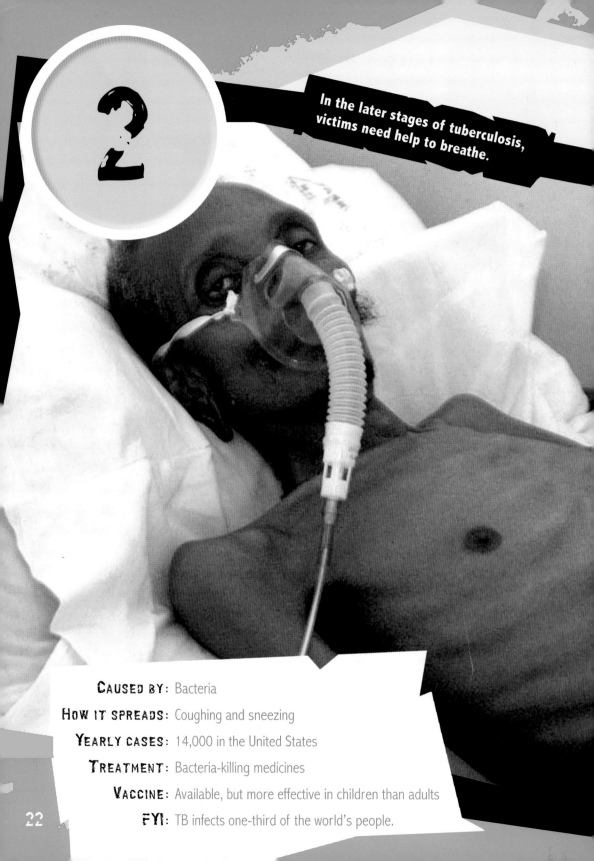

2

In the later stages of tuberculosis, victims need help to breathe.

CAUSED BY: Bacteria

HOW IT SPREADS: Coughing and sneezing

YEARLY CASES: 14,000 in the United States

TREATMENT: Bacteria-killing medicines

VACCINE: Available, but more effective in children than adults

FYI: TB infects one-third of the world's people.

TUBERCULOSIS

Tuberculosis was once the most deadly disease in the United States. In the 1940s, new medicines got TB under temporary control. But it's still a threat in many countries, especially poorer countries. Worldwide, nearly 2 million people die of tuberculosis each year.

TB spreads when infected people cough or sneeze. They release tiny germ-filled droplets into the air. Healthy people breathe in the germs. TB germs first attack the lungs. They work their way into the bloodstream and travel to the kidneys, spine, or brain.

One of the first symptoms is a cough that lasts longer than two weeks. The person also coughs up blood, feels tired, and doesn't want to eat.

Medicine is available to treat TB. But in poorer countries where TB is widespread, the medicine isn't widely available.

HIV/AIDS

1

Some AIDS patients get a form of skin cancer called Kaposi's sarcoma.

FULL NAME: Human Immunodeficiency Virus

HOW IT SPREADS: Through body fluids, such as blood

CASES: About 40,000 new cases in the United States each year

TREATMENT: Antiretroviral medicines

VACCINE: None

HIV is the virus that causes AIDS. AIDS itself doesn't kill. Instead, it weakens a person's immune system by attacking T cells. T cells are the parts of the blood that fight illnesses. When T cells are weakened, the person gets sick easily.

Doctors diagnosed the first case of AIDS in 1981. Since then, 20 million people have died worldwide. Another 38 million are infected with HIV. About 1 million of those people live in the United States.

There is no cure for HIV or AIDS, but medicines can keep it under control. But like most treatments for deadly diseases, these medicines are expensive. Many people can't afford them.

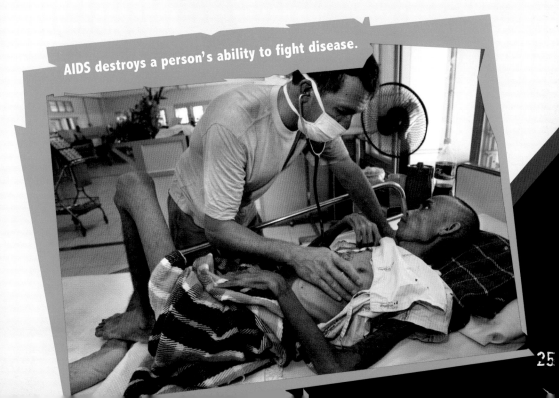
AIDS destroys a person's ability to fight disease.

DEADLIEST DISEASES

10

ANTHRAX

9

CANCER

PLAGUE

8

7

SMALLPOX

6

EBOLA

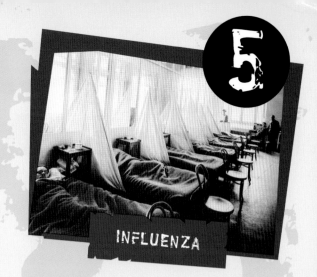

5

INFLUENZA

4

CHOLERA

MALARIA

3

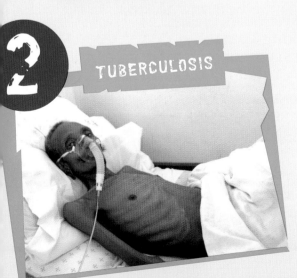

2

TUBERCULOSIS

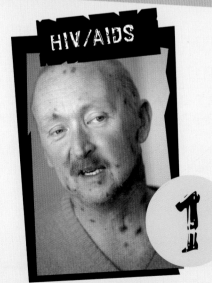

HIV/AIDS

1

27

UNDERSTANDING DISEASES

From bumps to bleeding to bursting buboes, diseases cause some nasty things to happen. Each disease is different, but they all have the potential to kill.

While many deadly diseases can't be prevented, there are things you can do to lower your risk. Eat nutritious food. Drink clean water. Wash your hands. Wear insect spray. Get vaccinated. If you're traveling to a faraway place, learn about the diseases in that country.

And if you don't feel well, see a doctor. Taking care of yourself is the best way to stop deadly diseases from taking control.

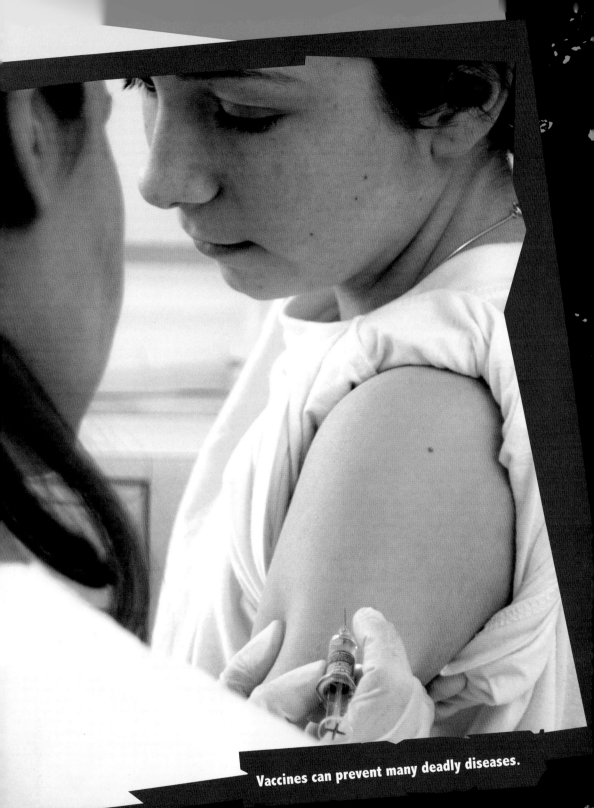

Vaccines can prevent many deadly diseases.

Glossary

bacteria (bak-TIHR-ee-uh)—tiny organisms that exist inside and around all living things; bacteria can cause diseases.

epidemic (ep-uh-DEM-ik)—a disease that spreads quickly

immune system (i-MYOON SISS-tuhm)—the parts of the body that protect it against disease and infection

parasite (PAIR-uh-site)—an animal or plant that needs to live on or inside another animal or plant to survive

tumor (TOO-mur)—an unhealthy mass of cells in the body

vaccine (vak-SEEN)—a shot of medicine that protects people against a disease

virus (VYE-ruhss)—a tiny particle that infects living things and causes diseases

READ MORE

Claybourne, Anna. *World's Worst Germs: Micro-organisms and Disease.* Fusion. Chicago: Raintree, 2005.

Friedlander, Mark P. *Outbreak: Disease Detectives at Work.* Minneapolis: Lerner, 2003.

Peters, Stephanie True. *The 1918 Influenza Pandemic.* Epidemic! New York: Benchmark Books, 2005.

Reed, Jennifer. *The AIDS Epidemic: Disaster and Survival.* Deadly Disasters. Berkeley Heights, N.J.: Enslow, 2005.

INTERNET SITES

FactHound offers a safe, fun way to find Internet sites related to this book. All of the sites on FactHound have been researched by our staff.

Here's how:

1. Visit *www.facthound.com*
2. Type in this special code **0736854525** for age-appropriate sites. Or enter a search word related to this book for a more general search.
3. Click on the **Fetch It** button.

FactHound will fetch the best sites for you!

INDEX